A Director's Guide

Managing knowledge in the Digital Age

HELPING DIRECTORS SUCCEED IN THE KNOWLEDGE-BASED ECONOMY

Editor, Director Publications: Tom Nash
Managing Editor: Lesley Shutte
Production Manager: Victoria Davies
Design: Halo Design
Commercial Director: Simon Seward
Managing Director: Andrew Main Wilson
Chairman: George Cox

Published for the Institute of Directors
and Computacenter
by Director Publications Ltd
116 Pall Mall London SW1Y 5ED

Editorial: 020 7766 8910
Production: 020 7766 8960
Sponsorship: 020 7766 8885
Copy sales: 020 7766 8766
Facsimile: 020 7766 8990

© Copyright January 2000
Director Publications Ltd

Price £9.95

YOURS TO HAVE AND TO HOLD
BUT NOT TO COPY

Director Publications Ltd
116 Pall Mall
London SW1Y 5ED

Kogan Page Ltd
120 Pentonville Road
London N1 9JN

©Director Publications Ltd 2000

British Library Cataloguing in Publication Data
A CIP record for this book is available from the British Library
ISBN 0 7494 3306 X

Printed and bound in Great Britain

Contents

@londonparistokyo

To serve financial customers anywhere, The Chase Manhattan Bank wanted a way to leverage IT assets everywhere. New business integration software from IBM is helping them unite IT systems in 83 markets into a single worldwide business platform for customers. And a powerful instrument of change for Chase. If you're looking for a powerful new way to shape technology to business strategy, visit www.ibm.com/software/big/uk/vision

Chase is an IBM e-business

Managing your most precious commodity

**George Cox, Director General,
Institute of Directors**

Knowledge management has become a major issue for every substantial organisation. The problem is that not everyone recognises this fact, or if they do, they do not know what to do about it.

It would be a mistake to regard "knowledge management" as simply a hyped-up term for something we have been doing for years. Things have changed, three in particular. Businesses have become much more knowledge-dependent; staff nowadays do not spend a lifetime with the same organisation; and modern technology has opened up enormous opportunities for capturing and sharing information. Indeed, it can be argued that, in the new Millennium, the exploitation of knowledge will become the major driving force for economic growth.

Every director, therefore, needs to understand the role that knowledge really plays within the business and also how technology can both share that resource across the workforce and tap into the vast knowledge sources of the outside world.

The issues are not all technical. There is the question to be faced of how you persuade, perhaps even incentivise, people to share knowledge. If knowledge is power, and determines an individual's value to the organisation, why should anyone willingly share it?

Moreover, if knowledge is such a precious asset, how does an organisation protect and retain what it has developed and owns?

Understanding of these issues is developing fast, just as the facilities offered by technology keep advancing. This Director's Guide is written specifically to put directors in the picture.

Transforming work in the Digital Age

Mike Norris, Chief Executive,
Computacenter

If today's organisations are to respond quickly to customer needs and improve their profitability, they can't afford to ignore one of their greatest assets – their knowledge. The information that resides in an organisation's people, processes and relationships, as unique to itself, constitutes an important competitive differentiator – which needs to be fully and efficiently utilised.

By providing the means for this information to be captured, stored and retrieved, information technology is pivotal to the basis of a sound knowledge management strategy. It has become even more important with the internet's *de facto* acceptance as the primary global communication platform, enabling information, wherever it resides, to be made quickly and easily accessible.

Computacenter has already established itself as a leading player in the internet sector through designing, implementing and supporting the IT platforms required to run internet technologies. In addition, over 400 customers are connected to our On-Trac e-business procurement system, while our e-business division, The iGroup, answers customers' demands for tailored e-business solutions and consultancy, allowing them to extract even greater value from their IT investments.

Although we can only estimate how the internet and the accompanying revolution in knowledge management will transform the century to come, it's right that, in this guide, we should take stock of what is already being achieved – and what it means to businesses today.

We are delighted to be working with the IoD on this Director's Guide to "Managing knowledge in the Digital Age".

IMAGINE IF YOU HAD INSTANT ACCESS TO YOUR ENTIRE COMPANY'S KNOWLEDGE.

Whatever business you're in, you'll recognise that success ultimately depends on the skills and knowledge of your people.

In the Digital Age, competitive advantage will be achieved by sharing and using your organisation's corporate 'memory', faster and more comprehensively than your competitors.

Microsoft's® partners are experienced in building cost-effective knowledge management solutions for UK companies that deliver genuine business value within realistic time-frames. So whether you are looking to improve your business planning, reduce time-to-market, manage customer relationships or enhance the skills of your employees, our partners' solutions - built on the Microsoft platform – will give you the flexibility for whatever the future may hold.

DIGITAL
NERVOUS
SYSTEM

To find out how our partners have helped companies such as BP, Guinness, Greenalls and Mothercare to release the knowledge inside their organisations call 0345 00 1000 ext 710 for the Microsoft Knowledge Management Executive Summary or visit www.microsoft.com/uk/knowledge/

BUSINESS EVOLUTION FOR THE DIGITAL AGE

Where do you want to go today?®

www.microsoft.com/uk/knowledge/

Chapter 1

A knowledge-driven economy

Knowledge management will be the key to success in the new millennium. Michael Johnson and Rob Tarling, both e-business consultants of The iGroup, the e-business division of Computacenter, stress that this applies not just to large corporates, but all companies

In the new millennium the driving force for economic growth will come from knowledge. We are entering a new digital age in which wealth will be created by those entrepreneurs who are most successful at using knowledge to deliver their existing products and services more effectively or – perhaps, even more importantly – to create the kind of new products and services that nobody has ever before imagined.

Three years ago, two-thirds of managers questioned in a KPMG survey felt knowledge management didn't have much to offer. Last year, only one in 20 said it was likely to be unimportant. Opinions rarely change so fast on business issues, suggesting that knowledge management could represent not just another consultants' catch-phrase but a new way of working that can help to deliver sustainable competitive advantage.

Governments, too, are noting the growing importance of knowledge management. The most recent White Paper on corporate competitiveness is called *Building a Knowledge-Driven Economy*. And the World Bank titled its 1998/1999 annual report *Knowledge for Development*. Likewise, Microsoft's Bill Gates, who can probably claim more than most to be the creator of the knowledge economy, says that companies must tap into all the knowledge of their employees if they want to survive. "The successful companies of the next decade will be the ones that use digital tools to reinvent the way they work," he says in his latest book *Business @ the Speed of Thought: Using a Digital Nervous System.*

So, to what extent is knowledge management changing how we do business? Consider a business icon of the previous century – Henry Ford, the creator of the car giant. When Henry built his first Model T in 1908, the question of knowledge wasn't much on his mind. He knew the car was going to be constructed on his innovative production line and that it would be painted one colour – black. A limited range of engineering and manufacturing skills kept Henry in business profitably.

Today, the Ford Motor Corporation needs far more. It needs to keep itself at the leading edge of a range of new technologies (that Henry could never have imagined). It needs knowledge about the new materials that will feature in car manufacture of the future, in the latest manufacturing techniques (including those used by its rivals). It also needs to know what its customers will want – not just today – but in 10 years' time.

But that's not all. Ford also needs a large amount of knowledge about the geo-political and environmental trends that will have a big impact on how the motor car industry develops in this new century. Today, Ford's ability to remain a major player in one of the world's largest and most competitive industries relies not just on its skill at building cars - but equally on its ability to understand what kind of cars customers will want to drive in a world that is becoming ever more congested and polluted. This represents a knowledge management challenge on a giant scale.

CHANGING THE NATURE OF BUSINESS

What is also important about the knowledge economy is that it is creating entirely new companies from nowhere. Consider, for example, all the Internet companies that have sprung into existence in the past ten years. Some like Yahoo!, the internet search engine, and Amazon.com, the on-line bookstore, experienced the kind of phenomenal growth in shareholder value – though not in profits – previously unknown in business history.

Yet companies in other industries, which ten years ago looked as though they might never change, have also begun to recognise that the knowledge economy will be a very different kind of place and are adapting accordingly. One example is Tesco, the supermarket chain. The company is rapidly moving from the pile-it-high, sell-it-cheap store that its founder Jack Cohen envisaged, to becoming a knowledge-centred business that can compete not only with other supermarkets but with other businesses in areas as diverse as financial services and petrol retailing. It's also become an Internet Service Provider (ISP) providing an easy way on to the World Wide Web (WWW) and is now offering customers the opportunity to order their groceries over the Net for home delivery, a service that had all but died out in Britain's grocery trade.

BUILDING CUSTOMER PROFILES

Tesco is adopting a very shrewd strategy for the knowledge economy. From a starting point where it knew little about the preferences of its individual customers, it's creating a competitive landscape where it can build a detailed profile of more customers as they switch to Internet shopping. Furthermore, by encouraging people to access the Internet through its "portal" it is in a powerful position to offer a range of other products and services with higher profit margins than groceries.

So those companies with a knowledge content in what they do – or that are specifically created in order to exploit the commercial value of knowledge – are in a strong position to become the turbo-charged value creators of the new millennium. Similarly, those companies that have never thought of themselves as knowledge-rich will be in a position to climb on this accelerating bandwagon if, like Tesco, they use enough imagination to devise innovative new business strategies.

Neither is the knowledge economy the sole preserve of the big beasts of the corporate jungle. Small and medium-sized enterprises (SMEs) are in a strong position to win some of the prizes. Indeed, if anything, they often possess qualities their larger competitors lack – the ability to think quickly and move fast, unburdened by corporate bureaucracy or ponderous decision-making processes.

SPEEDING AHEAD

As managing director of Microsoft in the UK, I am aware that senior executives in the UK are faced with many challenges as we enter the Digital Age. The extract from Bill Gates' book, **Business @ the Speed of Thought**, that follows illustrates some of the new challenges for business. It stresses that the new millennium will be about speed: speed of response to customers, speed of delivery of information, services or products and speed of adaptation to new markets and needs.

Of the assets that an organisation relies upon to respond in this new world, possibly the most important is its people. A lot has already been said about this field but Microsoft is focused on two things. First, defining the business value that organisations can derive from exploiting knowledge and therefore where to start. Second, we place an emphasis on empowering people with easier access to knowledge and providing them with the tools they need to be most effective.
– Neil Holloway, managing director of Microsoft in the UK

"Business is going to change more in the next ten years than it has in the last 50.

As I was preparing my speech for our first CEO summit in the spring of 1997, 1 was pondering how the digital age will fundamentally alter business. I wanted to go beyond a speech on dazzling technology advances and address questions that business leaders wrestle with all the time. How can technology help you run your business better? How will technology transform business? How can technology help make you a winner five or ten years from now?

If the 1980s were about quality and the 1990s were about reengineering, then the 2000s will be about velocity. About how quickly the nature of business will change. About how quickly business itself will be transacted. About how information access will alter the lifestyle of consumers and their expectations of business. Quality improvements and business process improvements will occur far faster. When the increase in velocity of business is great enough, the very nature of business changes. A manufacturer or retailer that responds to changes in sales in hours instead of weeks is no longer at heart a product company, but a service company that has a product offering.

These changes will occur because of a disarmingly simple idea: the flow of digital information. We've been in the Information Age for about 30 years, but because most of the information moving among businesses has remained in paper form, the process of buyers finding

SPEEDING AHEAD

sellers remains unchanged. Most companies are using digital tools to monitor their basic operations: to run their production systems; to generate customer invoices; to handle their accounting; to do their tax work. But these uses just automate old processes.

Very few companies are using digital technology for new processes that radically improve how they function, that give them the full benefit of all their employees' capabilities, and that give them the speed of response they will need to compete in the emerging high-speed business world. Most companies don't realise that the tools to accomplish these changes are now available to everyone.

Though at heart most business problems are information problems, almost no one is using information well.Too many senior managers seem to take the absence of timely information as a given. People have lived for so long without information at their fingertips that they don't realise what they're missing. One of the goals in my speech to the CEOs was to raise their expectations. I wanted them to be appalled by how little they got in the way of actionable information from their current IT investments. I wanted CEOs to demand a flow of information that would give them quick, tangible knowledge about what was really happening with their customers.

Even companies that have made significant investments in information technology are not getting the results they could be. What's interesting is that the gap is not the result of a lack of technology spending. In fact, most companies have invested in the basic building blocks: PCs for productivity applications; networks and electronic mail (e-mail) for communications; basic business applications.

The typical company has made 80 percent of the investment in the technology that can give it a healthy flow of information yet is typically getting only 20 per cent of the benefits that are now possible. The gap between what companies are spending and what they're getting stems from the combination of not understanding what is possible and not seeing the potential when you use technology to move the right information quickly to everyone in the company.

The key driver of this economy is technology. Computer technology has become both pervasive and powerful. Both qualities are essential for the knowledge economy. Pervasive means that all workers (within reason) who need computer technology now have access to it. The ubiquitous nature of the technology means that people can now work together from remote sites all round the world.

BETTER EQUIPPED, BETTER INFORMED

The power of today's computers also enables businesses to do things at a cost that was unimaginable just a decade ago. Moreover, in the last five years in particular, the Internet has made more information more accessible than at any previous time in history. Before our very eyes, it is literally transforming how we get information about everything – from tomorrow's flights to New York to delivery lead-times for obscure electronic components.

But it's not just the availability of technology that's important. The speed of change in business makes knowledge management essential. Companies rise and fall faster than ever before. Take Vodafone – a company that came from nowhere and has risen within a decade to become the second most valuable business in the UK. Conversely, there are firms that once found themselves at the pinnacle of their markets that have lost valuable ground at alarming speed. Furthermore, new technology and the internet is changing the rules of business, reshaping supply chains and creating new winners and losers. Direct Line, for example, has revolutionised the way insurance is sold.

THE NEED FOR CHANGE

In this climate, it's important that businesses change frequently in order to survive. In the early nineties, there was a fad for business re-engineering. This used radical reform of the way a business operated – usually by reorganising it on the basis of processes rather than functions – in order to win step-change benefits in performance. In the early days, those businesses that re-engineered first gained competitive advantage.

Today businesses are looking for something beyond re-engineering and, for many, that is knowledge management. In this climate, it's not surprising that "knowledge workers" are becoming increasingly important in the economy. This term applies not only to workers in solid knowledge industries such as computer software or business information publishing, but across the board. It's difficult to think of a job where the amount of time spent processing information is not rising.

Take the shop assistant. A few years ago, he or she would have handed over your groceries and taken your money. Today's assistant is likely to be operating a machine that also calculates loyalty points on a swipe card and presents you with offers based on your current points. The main feature of this new work is to collect customer data that can be turned into essential information about customer preferences and shopping trends. This is vital knowledge for future decision-making.

In the light of this seismic shift in the nature of economic activity, some of the traditional rules of business are changing in the new knowledge economy. For example, who previously heard of companies giving away free products? But some Internet Service Providers, such as Dixon Group's Freeserve, do this as a way to build market-share and create traffic through their portal – which then becomes commercially attractive to advertisers.

TELESCOPING TIMESCALES

In the knowledge economy, traditional time-scales are shortened. The ready availability of knowledge and the technology that enables people to use it effectively, makes it possible – although not necessarily easier – to launch new products more quickly. Take the example of Ford, mentioned earlier. By using knowledge more effectively, it has shortened the typical timescale for launching a new car from five years to two.

But it's also possible to launch new digital products and services much more quickly. Some financial services companies such as banks and insurance companies, for example, boast that they can launch a new insurance policy or bank account within days to forestall a competitor's move or meet sudden customer demand.

On top of all this, many companies are using the knowledge economy to search for ways to provide value-added products or services. This is particularly important for a company that is in a market which is highly competitive, perhaps over-supplied, and

KNOWLEDGE ASSETS WITH VALUE

Knowledge sources like these could represent important revenue-generating opportunities for many companies:

Brands	Management tools and techniques
Consultancy and advice	Manufacturing processes
Copyrights	Market intelligence
Customer information	Patents
Design rights	Proprietary technologies
Distribution networks	R&D know-how
Libraries/archives	Royalties
Licences	Software
Mailing/telephone lists	Training materials
Management methodologies	Web site/other Internet presence

whose margins are constantly under pressure. Sony, for example, has repositioned itself in the last few years, from being a mere provider of electronic goods, such as TVs and Walkmans (albeit a new concept product, which it invented), to a vertically integrated company that provides content and services, such as computer games, and transmission facilities as well as its consumer goods.

YOUR FUTURE DEPENDS ON IT

In essence, there are two over-arching lessons from the knowledge economy that directors need to take on board. The first is that, whatever the business, managing knowledge will be increasingly important in developing it successfully in the future. It's a big mistake to believe that knowledge management is only relevant to high-tech companies in industries such as software and the Internet. Every company has knowledge deeply embedded inside it – knowledge that it can use to run the business better.

That first message is very simple: what you know is valuable in making more profit from what you do. But, in order to harness and use what you know more effectively, you will need to use some of the knowledge management strategies and techniques described later in this guide.

Second, what you know may be more than just a way of managing your existing business better. The knowledge in your company may represent commercial possibilities in its own right. Every company is different, but most will have some of the key knowledge assets listed in the table opposite.

Any one of them could represent opportunities for developing additional income. Dow Chemical, for example, generated an extra £85m in revenues and savings within two years by managing its huge portfolio of patents more actively.

We've already explored how incredibly exhilarating the knowledge economy is going to be. Fortunes can be made, if not overnight, certainly within months, when an innovative idea captures the imagination of the public – or, sometimes, venture capitalists. The knowledge economy will be a place for directors who can think laterally and look at their companies in different ways. It will also be a place where added pressure will be put on directors to make decisions quickly and take risks.

It could also be quite a frightening place, especially for those companies that find it difficult to change. For these, extinction may be closer than they realise. When the whole rules of a market can effectively be rewritten overnight, there is no room for companies that refuse to move forward.

Even so, the overall prognosis is bright. It seems likely – although economists argue about this endlessly – that the technological innovation of the knowledge economy is one of the key drivers of the economic growth which Britain and the United States has seen since the mid-nineties (the US sooner than the UK). If knowledge – rather than raw materials and manufacturing – is the new driver of wealth creation, there is no reason why thousands of businesses shouldn't benefit.

Chapter 2

What is knowledge management?

To benefit from knowledge management, a company must secure proper IT support for its business processes and have good corporate communications and human resource policies. Peter Bartram, business and technology writer, reports

T S Eliot, author of *Old Possum's Book of Practical Cats*, spotted the problem years ago. "Where is the wisdom? Lost in the knowledge," he wrote. "Where is the knowledge? Lost in the information." Unfortunately, Eliot never came up with a solution. But, then, he'd never heard of knowledge management.

Today, the problem is rather different. Most directors have heard of it – but not all of them are quite sure exactly what it is. When the *International Consultants' Guide* asked managers in 81 companies to define knowledge management, they came up with a range of explanations from "data warehousing" to the grandiloquent "strategic gathering of information for development, innovation and administration."

From a practical perspective, finding a neat form of words to define knowledge management is less important than understanding the core concepts wrapped inside it. Essentially, the principles behind knowledge management are not that much different from managing physical assets. Every company manages assets such as buildings, machinery and vehicles. Most devote considerable time and expertise to making sure they squeeze the maximum amount of value out of each. Yet, while this is important, these physical assets often have less potential to deliver new value to a business than the knowledge inside it, which is often not managed anywhere nearly so vigorously.

These assets exist in a physical form. When something goes wrong with them – a fire in a factory, a crash with a company car – it's easy to see the damage done. Moreover, because the assets are physical, it's also easier to envision ways of working them harder. Think of the time companies spend figuring out ways to pack more stock into a warehouse or increase the throughput on a machine.

Exactly the same kinds of issues arise with knowledge. If a valued employee leaves the company, the knowledge that employee possesses goes too. When management consultancy KPMG asked companies to identify the downside of a valued employee quitting, nearly half referred to lost knowledge of best practice in a specific operational area. More than four out of ten identified damage to a key client relationship. As many as one in seven lost information vital to running the business or "significant revenue".

HARVESTING VALUE FROM KNOWLEDGE

However, knowledge management is not just a damage-limitation exercise. Its core purpose is to manage the knowledge in order to harvest more value from it. Failure to do so may result in loss of competitive edge, missed business opportunities and a shortfall on profit. So, if it's important to manage company knowledge as least as effectively as the physical assets, how do you do it?

The starting point is to recognise that more or less every company has three kinds of knowledge inside it. These are:

- *Explicit;*

- *Tacit;*

- *Potential.*

The most obvious is "explicit knowledge", which is information recorded in documents or residing in computer systems. Companies are overloaded with it. In fact, the research organisation IDC estimates that 80 per cent of all organisational knowledge resides in unstructured documents. Moreover, people are creating new knowledge every hour of every day.

The second type is tacit knowledge. This is information that people hold in their heads but do not feel the need to write down. It includes knowledge about the best way to do something, which only comes from experience. The problem with tacit knowledge is that it's only ever available to the person who possesses it unless there is an explicit effort to record it.

Finally, there is "potential knowledge". Every company has a mass of raw data in its computer systems about customers, products and markets which never gets used. It just sits there unanalysed, refusing to give up its secrets. Yet often the secrets it holds could provide new business insights that might reveal a better way of working, a new product opportunity or an innovative strategy for tackling a competitive market.

Harnessing any one of these kinds of information can prove difficult as information resides in different formats, in multiple places. Further problems often arise because the data is not integrated effectively across all the different systems within an organisation. And knowledge workers often need to work with people outside their immediate group: individuals within the same company elsewhere in the world, from a partner company, and even suppliers and customers.

FACTORS IN EFFECTIVE MANAGEMENT

While there is no easy way to solve this problem, a company can vastly increase the value it harvests from its knowledge by properly managing a combination of factors. The starting point is always people – they create knowledge and often hoard it, either in their own offices or in their heads. Therefore, a shift in culture must lie at the heart of any knowledge management strategy. The idea that "knowledge is power" is well known and – unfortunately for some companies – well exploited by many of its employees. Refusing to share information is a way for workers to boost their importance (real or imagined) and keep themselves in decision-making loops.

This is a tough problem but can be tackled by creating a cooperative teamworking culture in which people need to share information at least with their immediate working colleagues.

CLOSING A KNOWLEDGE GAP

Eyretel, a fast-growing company that sells digital voice recording technology for use in call centres, was growing so fast it had hit a knowledge gap

The problem was that its best sales people – those with most experience – were constantly out-performing its newer recruits. This was causing expense – and occasional embarrassment – to the company.

When rookie sales people went out on calls they often had to take an engineer with them to explain the technical details of Eyretel's complex products. If the rookies went without an engineer, they risked being bowled out by a tough question from the customer. "I'll get back to you on that one," is never an impressive reply.

Nathan George, Eyretel's global marketing manager, was determined to find a way of enabling the company's most inexperienced sales people to perform as well as its best. He consulted Don Fuller, managing director of cotoco, a knowledge management solutions company based in Fareham.

Fuller's solution was to capture the knowledge of the best sales people and package it in a computer system that could be delivered to every sales person through a laptop.

Today, Eyretel's sales force – marketing its products in 80 countries – go into pitches with the laptop knowledge system. This provides a media library to help Eyretel's sales people to customise presentations to customers' precise needs. There are proposal templates to make customer presentations more professional. And there's also a library of training material, including in-depth information on all Eyretel's products and services.

As a result of closing the knowledge gap between its most and least effective sales people, Eyretel no longer has to send engineers with the rookies. And, using the system, new sales staff can come up to speed much more quickly than before. Eyretel's chief executive Roger Keenan is unequivocal about the benefits of knowledge management: "This is by far the most professional piece of marketing we've ever produced."

Once a knowledge hoarder learns to swap information with people he knows, he may become more willing to share information widely. Some companies have looked at remunerating knowledge workers on the basis of team rather than individual performance.

While this can focus minds and change attitudes, it is a complex issue in its own right.

What certainly helps is if the processes used within a company – the second key element in the knowledge management equation – make it easy for people to share knowledge. It can be particularly effective where there are natural connections – between people or teams working on the same business process, developing a new product or solving a customer's problem. It is also important to make sharing information easier across different functions within the company.

Mapping a process can help everybody to understand where the linkages are and how information should flow around. Mapping will also increase the amount of knowledge about the process and highlight ways in which it can be improved – capturing some of that "tacit knowledge" about how people do their work.

HAVING THE RIGHT TECHNOLOGY

Managing the processes effectively almost always depends on having the right technology to hand. This is the third critical element of a knowledge management solution. Large companies face the technical issue of exchanging information across legacy systems. Meanwhile, small and medium-sized enterprises often suffer from a lack of sufficient IT expertise – or investment cash – in the company to create the kind of systems that would make it easier to retrieve essential information. This can only be solved by looking again at investment priorities and the potential pay-back from knowledge management.

In summary, the purpose of using knowledge more effectively in business is to create more value. More companies now recognise the value of knowledge and some even refer to the contribution of knowledge to their business success in the annual report. With a positive approach, there's no reason why – as T S Eliot gloomily suggested – knowledge should remain lost in information.

Chapter 3

Developing knowledge strategies

A company's knowledge management strategies should be based on the systematic analysis of how knowledge enables it to achieve its objectives. Ashley Braganza, lecturer and programme director at Cranfield School of Management, offers a framework for businesses to follow

This chapter provides directors with a pragmatic framework for developing knowledge management strategies that are linked inextricably to the organisation's business strategy.

ESTABLISHING A FRAMEWORK

Such a framework is needed now for a number of reasons. First, many companies have developed a knowledge management strategy only to find it remains filed away in the IT director's top drawer. This is often due to a noticeable gap between the business strategy and the knowledge management strategy.

Second, the investment in knowledge management, in terms of senior managers' time and budgets, should lead to business benefits. However, recent research indicates organisations gain insignificant benefits, which signifies the demise of knowledge management.

A third reason is that knowledge management experts are rapidly becoming a feature of the organisational landscape, with departments forming under the direction of an IT director supported by knowledge managers. Yet these roles quickly lose their relevance when people disregard knowledge and its management as a part of their "day job".

Let's begin by clarifying at two widely held views about knowledge management. The first concerns the different levels at which knowledge management can be said to reside. The following three levels are identified:

- *Industry;*

- *Organisation;*

- *Individual.*

These levels are useful for the purposes of gathering, creating, sharing and deploying knowledge, but their relevance for the purposes of developing a knowledge strategy is limited.

Knowledge, at the level of industry, is usually publicly available, and consequently its strategic potential is negligible; individual knowledge tends to be fragmented and insular; and the organisation is often too indefinite and amorphous for knowledge to be specified. Therefore, it is essential to identify a unit of knowledge analysis relevant to developing knowledge strategies that can be linked to the business strategy. This chapter proposes the business process (as defined overleaf) is an appropriate unit of analysis.

The second issue concerns the nature of knowledge management projects initiated by organisations. Typically, the outputs of these projects are an intranet, data warehouse or the creation of an organisational culture that values knowledge.

While such projects are important to managing knowledge they, of and by themselves, constitute only one element of knowledge management, namely establishing an infrastructure that is conducive to exploiting knowledge.

Much of the research evidence suggests that current knowledge management projects yield limited benefits in the short term. This is hardly surprising, as the aim of most knowledge management projects is to create an appropriate infrastructure. Infrastructure-building projects rarely tend to deliver immediate results.

Hence, it is necessary to develop knowledge management strategies that enhance the exploitation and infrastructure aspects of knowledge.

DEVELOPING YOUR KNOWLEDGE MANAGEMENT STRATEGY

The framework consists of four inter-related elements: strategic direction, business processes, knowledge exploitation, and knowledge infrastructure. The first two elements establish the business needs, or the demand, for knowledge. The latter two form the supply of knowledge to fulfil the business needs.

Strategic direction

There are a plethora of techniques for designing a business strategy. Two schools of thought have particularly influenced strategy formulation. The analytical school guides managers to analyse their industry and identify a strategic position for the organisation. The strategy sets out how the organisation, over time, will reach its chosen position.

More recently, managers have been asked to identify their organisation's core competencies. These enable the organisation to change the industry's competitive rules or create an entirely new basis of competition.

An aspect of strategy that is often neglected is the identification and prioritisation of stakeholders. These include customers, suppliers, regulators, shareholders, and employees. Stakeholders have a degree of power over whether or not the organisation's business strategy is achieved. They also have expectations of the organisation and where these are unfulfilled, can use their influence to frustrate the organisation from achieving its business objectives.

Business processes

At a strategic level, business processes arise from and fulfil stakeholders' expectations. Consequently, processes deliver the organisation's strategy. Each process is self-renewing in relation to changes in the external environment. For example, where a stakeholder's expectation changes the business process adapts to meet the new expectation.

At an operational level, business processes integrate activities performed in different functions to satisfy the stakeholders' expectations.

Knowledge exploitation

As discussed elsewhere in the guide, knowledge can be explicit or tacit in nature. Explicit knowledge is contained in documents and information systems and is structured, widely disseminated and easily accessible. Tacit knowledge, which is crucial for innovation and strategic success, is embodied within people. It is a set of beliefs that individuals forge from their subjective views of the world and their personal experiences.

The content and nature of tacit and explicit knowledge varies for each business process. It is essential, therefore, to develop a knowledge exploitation strategy for each business process. For example, a car manufacturer has an order fulfilment process and a product development process.

The strategy to exploit knowledge in each process will be different. The knowledge exploitation strategy for the order fulfilment process may identify high levels of explicit knowledge. This could entail implementing an automated ordering system that is integrated with stock information, production plans, billing systems and delivery performance measurements.

The knowledge exploitation strategy for the product development process might suggest tacit knowledge as being more critical. The nature of the tacit knowledge required in the two processes is also different. In the order fulfilment process, tacit knowledge relates to people's capability to implement integrated systems and organisational changes quickly. In the product development process, tacit knowledge might include people being capable of interpreting fashion trends and translating these into unique design features for specific car models.

In addition to specifying the content and nature of knowledge in each process, knowledge exploitation strategies also indicate the following elements of each business process:

- *The modes of sharing the explicit and tacit knowledge, eg. persons-to-person, person-to-information system and vice versa, and information system-to-information system;*

- *The governance "rules" that enable knowledge to be generated, used, embedded, transferred, and deployed from one person or group to another in the same process and across processes;*

■ *The organisational changes needed to implement the knowledge exploitation strategy.*

Once an organisation has created knowledge exploitation strategies, it can turn its attention to the infrastructure required to support these strategies.

Knowledge infrastructure

The knowledge infrastructure strategy is created from two perspectives:

■ *Technological;*

■ *Cultural.*

The technological perspective includes identifying appropriate systems that may include integrated databases, data warehouses and mining tools, an intranet, and the use of the internet.

The cultural perspective suggests issues that ensure people perceive knowledge management to be an integral part of their role, and have mechanisms that reinforce the exploitation of knowledge. These mechanisms include:

■ *Making individual's responsible for sharing knowledge with colleagues;*

■ *Making knowledge exploitation part of each individual's annual assessment criteria; and*

■ *Providing people with a common language so that knowledge can be transferred between people.*

The extent of cultural change is based upon the requirements of the knowledge exploitation strategy for each process. So, rather than attempt to change the culture of the whole organisation, managers need only focus their efforts on adapting the culture of each process, so that each one achieves business benefits from tacit and explicit knowledge.

BENEFITS OF ALIGNING STRATEGIES

The alignment of business strategy and knowledge management strategies, both exploitation and infrastructure, brings several benefits. First, tacit and explicit knowledge that is necessary to implement the business strategy is identified and managed for each business process that satisfies stakeholders' expectations.

Second, the knowledge management strategies are likely to require strategic and operational organisational changes. Some of these changes may be radical in nature. By explicitly linking the knowledge management strategies to the business strategy it becomes difficult for people to avoid implementing the organisational changes. This makes it less likely that the knowledge strategies remain in the IT director's drawer.

Third, managers can identify business critical knowledge within each process and, hence, can focus on areas of the business where knowledge yields significant benefits.

Finally, knowledge management strategies derived from business processes support people's day-to-day activities. This makes knowledge relevant to people at all levels in the organisation and prevents knowledge experts from becoming distanced from their colleagues.

SUMMARY

This chapter presents a framework that ensures knowledge management strategies are aligned to the business strategy. It introduces the notion of knowledge exploitation strategies and a knowledge infrastructure strategy, and suggests that organisations develop both types of strategies.

The conclusion of this is that the creation of a single, all-encompassing knowledge management strategy is insufficient for the purposes of gaining business benefits from knowledge. The framework establishes business processes as the bridge between the business strategy and the knowledge management strategies and, hence, makes knowledge relevant to people across the company.

Chapter 4

Learning in context

Directors need to identify the different dimensions of learning within their organisations. Edward C Gonsalves, of the Centre for Strategy & Policy at the Open University Business School and Dr Daniel Summerfield, IoD Professional Development Executive, explain

There is an increasing realisation that knowledge management is critical to corporate success. The realisation comes as environmental events force senior executives into new ways of thinking about their businesses. For instance, we know that:

■ *The collective intellectual capital of organisations has been sorely under-utilised in the strategic process;*

■ *Pushing ahead with change programmes in the face of institutional and personal dogma damages enterprise to varying degrees;*

■ *Vital strategic alignment cannot be "sold" effectively unless divergent perceptions of stakeholders/players have been reconciled;*

■ *Static competitive advantage is ruined by persistent innovation.*

To accompany this increasing interest in business strategy new change management disciplines have been developed. Learning disciplines represent a basic toolkit that allow for knowledge management and behavioural change.

In addition, research by the IoD and Open University Business School has demonstrated that senior executives in small and medium-sized enterprises (SMEs) with strong innovation and customer focus credentials have significantly stronger orientations to organisational learning than those who are less predisposed to innovation and customer focus.

LEARNING THROUGH ACTION

The processes of acquiring and applying organisational knowledge need not be separate. The integration of workplace action and experiential learning is an essential prerequisite to competitiveness. Organisational learning can be viewed as the process through which knowledge growth, change and application can take place.

The multi-dimensional approach to organisational learning discussed in this chapter considers the activity of learning across a range of knowledge management needs and is accessible to SMEs.

INDIVIDUAL LEARNING

Individuals will tend to work in the same way until they experience a breakdown in their circumstances. This can happen because their expectations are not met, or because the external situation has changed. In order to move forward individuals often need to reflect on the actions they may take to overcome their difficulties. It is during these periods of reflection that opportunities arise for developing company learning initiatives.

There are particularly useful opportunities to understand best practices in those processes of workplace learning, whereby the individual personally solves contextually relevant problems. Here the individual brings to bear issue-specific know-how (eg. partner-client relationship management in law firms). Instances of reflective practice range from difficult to observe and measure intuitions, to more prolonged and explicit forms of knowledge application. People who would benefit from experiencing such action include newly hired apprentices who lack issue-specific knowledge and longer-serving employees who are being challenged to change thinking and/or behaviour. In the dynamic workplace then, no individual is able to totally determine what constitutes needed knowledge. The individual practitioner experiences a process of constant learning.

SOCIAL LEARNING

Much of the work reported on learning organisations draws on concepts from the field of individual learning. In formal organisations, other members and groups provide an important social context for the learning process. Even if people are the basic learning unit, it is essential to understand the collective process that links them to each other and the organisation.

Understanding the process through which groups learn, how they combine individual knowledge and beliefs into shared knowledge structures and take co-ordinated action is important. Acknowledging how individuals interpret and integrate shared understandings that guide collective actions is equally critical.

We can see how individual and group learning differ when we consider aspects of organisational learning that are currently being developed and implemented in companies. Increasingly these activities are also accessible to SMEs via technological media such as electronic newsletters and intranet discussion forums.

Organisational memory

This is a repository – be it archival or ritual in nature – that preserve intentions, processes, mechanisms and solutions from the organisation's past. They may hold accounts of critical events and key actors. Informal networks are a rich source of organisational memory.

Learning histories

Related to the organisational memory are learning histories. These are either written or recorded documents that are disseminated to help an organisation become better aware of its own learning effort. The history includes not just action and results reports, but also the underlying assumptions and reactions of a variety of people (including people who neither supported, nor were involved in the learning effort). No one individual view, not even that of senior managers, can encompass more than a fraction of what really goes on in a complex project. This reality is reflected in the learning history.

Recently at the Open University's Knowledge Media Institute, research has demonstrated how work teams evolve their own means of communication, judgement and negotiation in building a socially "constructed" domain of organisational practice. Team vocabularies, practices, customs and conventions develop so as to allow members a common understanding during complex task accomplishment.

The use of teams and project groups as the primary work unit is widespread in firms. The notion of individuals being immersed in "communities of practice" while being personally engaged in situated actions, provides a perspective from which to evaluate and support this dimension of workplace activity. Yet this dimension is one of the most misunderstood aspects of knowledge management and development.

A crucial part of this work has concentrated on how groups of individuals adopt "non-canonical" means to achieve "canonical" objectives. Canons represent explicit and codified organisational knowledge. They are collections of general laws, rules and principles that formally guide organisational behaviour. Non-canonical practices are equally important, but are rarely found in a company's documentation and formal procedures. They are primarily implicit, informal and observed through an organisation's non-textual communication channels, eg. chatting in the corridor.

A common example of non-canonical learning is reflected in the experience of field service staff in numerous technologically intensive enterprises (from software engineering firms to component manufacturers' suppliers). Service work is commonly thought of as the fixing of broken machines, computer code, etc. To support this work senior executives typically sponsor the provision of corporate documentation (canons) that directs field staff through to feasible problem solutions. Little recognition is given to how staff improvisation can be supported in the varied, idiosyncratic situations that they frequently experience. Knowledge is predominantly perceived as fixed.

In reality, however, field staff also diagnose problems through discussion with the user and by exchanging stories or ideas with their co-workers.

The changing and challenging nature of fieldwork requires practitioners to learn as a community through "narrative". This narrative process prepares staff to tell others of their experience, either in asking for help, telling of a new problem, or telling of stories about interesting problems. Through this social learning practice, they create knowledge that is non-canonical and emergent in nature. Over time some of these non-canonical practices become formalised as "best practice" and innovation.

MANAGING THE TENSION

The table overleaf highlights some of the tensions that senior executives will need to address when managing the stable-dynamic nature of organisational knowledge. The tensions are symptomatic of the differences between the individual and social knowledge construction processes described above. That is, the difference between the dimensions of individual and collective learning. Directors will need to devote considerable resources to identifying the relationship between these dimensions.

LEARNING AND CHANGE

Given the above dichotomy of interpretation any change programme adopted by a company will also have to pay close attention to the type of learning desired or currently in practice. While much knowledge and belief change is forced down from the top, another key influence is experimental learning where new experiences lead to a change in beliefs or understandings, as opposed to anticipatory learning where changes in beliefs lead to behavioural change.

If experimental learning is to occur it is important that beliefs are suspended long enough to let experience take hold. In contrast many organisations adopt a forced learning model whereby individuals are told to change. Although individuals often comply with these mandates, they often do not understand or buy into change. As soon as the edict is removed, or management changes, they often revert to type. Blocked learning occurs when other beliefs override the situation, such as: "I know the customer is always right, but I can't take this kind of abuse."

So, although intent may be present, habitual behaviours may prevent appropriate learning from taking place. Organisations work with familiar procedures and patterns which are habits of the "corporate mind", and are reinforced by structures and systems.

Individual and social knowledge		
CONCEPT	KNOWLEDGE AS CONSTRUCTED BY INDIVIDUALS	KNOWLEDGE CONSTRUCTED SOCIALLY
Knowledge perceived as:	Growing Finite Iterative Certain	Developing Infinite Interactive Doubtful
The 'world' (eg. markets, customers, competitors, etc.)	Pre-exists	Constituted
'Truth'	Unified: problem solution	Multiple: problem plausibility
Analysis	Of system/structure	Of stories and argument
Need to find/ discover	What different problems staff see	How staff come to see the same problem differently
Manager needs to surface conflict	Over-problem	Over understanding

Changing habits of the corporate mind is very difficult. It requires practice and repeated experience; a recognition of the need to change; a recognition of existing habits; and a conscious effort to co-ordinate habits across boundaries.

Increasingly, it is argued that in the emerging knowledge economy the key to competitive advantage at the enterprise level will be access to intellectual capital. In the main this will reside with the individual. Competitive advantage at the individual level is based on know-how, ie. "knowledge is power". The problem for management is how to create an organisation that is willing to share if most of its people are willing to learn, but not too many are motivated to teach or share. This chapter suggests frameworks for assessing learning within organisations.

Chapter 5

The people factor

A successful knowledge management strategy will motivate people to generate ideas and share their experience. Dr Mike Bagshaw, director of Trans4mation consultancy stresses that the key lies in good communications

Intangible assets (know-how, brand and processes) are gaining ground over tangibles (property plant and equipment). Research carried by out the Brookings Institute has identified that tangible assets represented 62.3 per cent of company value in 1982, but only 37.9 per cent in 1992. In 1996, Microsoft had only a fraction of the tangible assets of IBM ($930m as against $16.6bn), yet had a market value of $85.5bn, as against IBM's $70.7bn.

Organisations are typically unaware of the vast potential of their people. Often, the knowledge needed for the products and services is not even part of formal procedures, but stays in the shadows. Communication techniques have evolved to a new level, with e-mail, intranet, and video and audio conferencing use becoming ever more widespread. However, companies still lack systems and cultures to ensure knowledge sharing and transfer.

With the aid of IT, mutual sharing can lead to knowledge expanding like a volcano. The lava from this volcano is alive. It sees and responds to change, involves others, and seeks out the best possible way to adapt. It's an organic, not a mechanical, process. The very word "organisation" suggests organs being arranged to make a whole, but the way this is done has to change.

The tradition is to have the top organ as the head, and others beneath. The head has the knowledge to control the others. That can't work when knowledge rushes in on all sides like it does today. It has to be filtered from all directions, not be channelled through the top.

How do we choose from the vast amount of information available? We need to decide what will really make a difference, and concentrate on that. How we focus is important, and not just for the immediate situation. Our focus now shapes how things will be. When the flow of new information was less excessive, we tended to let experts do the focusing for us. Today, we need to avoid this dependency, find our own focus and share all our knowledge.

Jack Welch, CEO of General Electric, talks of "freeing" people. He said: "If you want to get the benefit of everything employees have, you have to free them – make everybody a participant. Everybody has to know everything, so they can make the right decisions for themselves."

This means a loss of status for experts who tend to cling on to their knowledge. One way to make them value sharing is to change the reward system that traditionally favours the old-style expert. Lotus Development, for example, now includes knowledge sharing in performance evaluation.

ROADBLOCKS TO KNOWLEDGE SHARING

Ideally a company behaves like a chrysalis. As it unfolds, it learns. People with a keen interest in the same thing make discoveries that are far too exciting to keep to themselves. Knowledge spreads as they seek to amalgamate their different finds. Motivation is strong because people feel involved and that they belong. This fulfils a fundamental emotional need and increases their desire to contribute. Such a group of people who feel they belong will be a rich source of knowledge and experience, and they will give freely. Unfortunately, traditional hierarchical cultures tend to stifle this process by reinforcing restrictive attitudes and behaviours like:

■   *Focusing on short-term goals and the job in hand, rather than the overall purpose;*

■   *Fostering an "us and them" siege mentality;*

■   *Failing to accept the extent to which the culture's problems are self-inflicted;*

■   *Ignoring subtle changes in the business environment until it's too late;*

■   *Failing to systematically manage and review their learning;*

■   *Engaging in business limiting "turf" politics, cliques, and defensive tactics;*

■   *Looking for scapegoats, rather than learning from mistakes.*

These "roadblocks" often reflect deep-rooted attitudes, which are notoriously difficult to change head-on.

APPRECIATIVE INQUIRY

We need a whole new way of looking at organisations to move forward. Appreciative Inquiry is one concept, pioneered by Professor Suresh Srivastva and Assistant Professor David Cooperrider of Organisational Behaviour at Case Western Reserve University, Cleveland, Ohio.

They argue that organisations, like works of art, can be looked at in many ways. Thinking in terms of problems tends to bring with it feelings of helplessness. Building on that which is already being done well is more motivating. It involves finding the best examples, understanding how they came about, and amplifying those processes. Sharing this kind of knowledge, using the latest technology, will liberate people's potential. The collective choices of all employees will create the future of the organisation.

Appreciative Inquiry seeks out stories embracing business-enhancing themes. New technology makes it easier to disseminate these stories, which are then woven into narratives, which shape the future: the future we anticipate is the future we create.

CHANGE AND DIVERSITY

IT spreads and amplifies the effects of Appreciative Inquiry further. However, this democratisation of knowledge will be resisted by many. For a company's knowledge management strategy to succeed, it must dismantle all barriers of resistance and the tenacity of dated assumptions. Nobody has a monopoly on the best ideas. Of course, there will be disagreement. If everybody agreed, innovation would stop. Properly managed, disagreement is a hotbed for creativity.

Companies need to create a culture where knowledge is valued, whatever its source. This can mean fundamentally rethinking how individuals are seen in relation to the organisation. It also means recognising that knowledge sharing will bring more, and better, collective power. The demands of global competitiveness and the speed of change means we have to achieve levels of collaboration, teamwork, and direct communication we never dreamed possible. To do this, we have to optimise our personal resources.

EMOTIONAL INTELLIGENCE

Positive emotions can make a real difference to the quality of decision-making, leadership, customer loyalty, creativity and innovation. Daniel Goleman, behavioural psychologist and author of *Emotional Intelligence – why it can matter more than IQ*, argues persuasively that emotionally intelligent behaviour is the key to competitive advantage in the knowledge driven economy.

He defines emotional intelligence as: "...the capacity for recognising our own feelings and those of others, for motivating ourselves, and for managing emotions well in ourselves and in our relationships." In the context of knowledge management, this means the following business-enhancing behaviour:

■ *Confidence in finding knowledge people inside and outside the organisation;*

■ *Automatically considering who else will benefit from this knowledge so the business can move forward, and collaborating with others to create new knowledge and solutions;*

■ *Suspending assumptions and engaging in open dialogue;*

■ *Believing in the value of giving first, before expecting to receive;*

■ *Finding opportunities for, not barriers against, collaborative effort;*

■ *Not believing that sharing knowledge means losing something;*

■ *Being committed to lifelong learning;*

- *Recognising that their own knowledge and experience is a precious asset that can add value to the business;*

- *Genuinely caring – enough to say the worst – giving honest feedback and challenging others to be the best they can be.*

Conversely, anger, fear, exclusion and uncertainty, are powerful emotions that limit business. More than ever companies cannot afford to lose customers by exhibiting attitudes of indifference, lose significant working days through stress-related absence, have change programmes fail because of people's low morale, resistance, cynicism and self-preservation at the cost of collaborative working.

THE NEED FOR NETWORK LEADERSHIP

Within this new working environment, there needs to be a different type of leadership. Peter Senge, senior lecturer at Massachusetts Institute of Technology and chief executive officer of the Society for Organisational learning, argues that a new form of leader is emerging in the Knowledge Company – the network leader.

These individuals do not exercise the power of position and status. They develop broad alliances and partnerships across organisational boundaries. They are natural "seed carriers" of new ideas and build and orchestrate communities of learning and knowledge exchange. We need to legitimise and value these individuals. They will play a crucial support role in filtering and prioritising the flood of information in the changing work environment.

The rewards for the culture shift outlined in this chapter can be enormous. Chevron Oil saved $150m per year in energy and field expenses by sharing knowledge of skills in energy management from international plants. Knowledge sharing is a primary asset of any business. The cost of not sharing in the global market can be expensive, and potentially catastrophic.

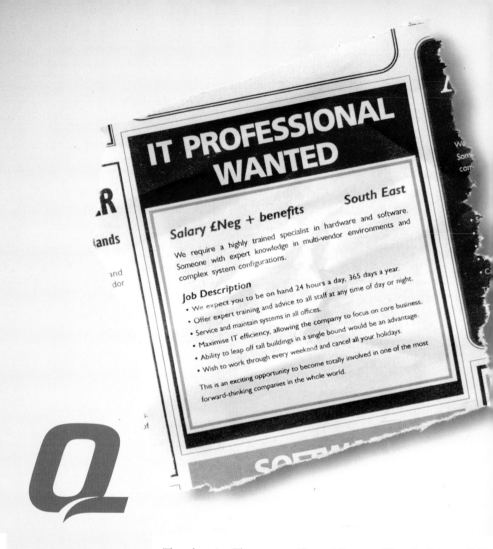

IT PROFESSIONAL WANTED

Salary £Neg + benefits **South East**

We require a highly trained specialist in hardware and software. Someone with expert knowledge in multi-vendor environments and complex system configurations.

Job Description

- We expect you to be on hand 24 hours a day, 365 days a year.
- Offer expert training and advice to all staff at any time of day or night.
- Service and maintain systems in all offices.
- Maximise IT efficiency, allowing the company to focus on core business.
- Ability to leap off tall buildings in a single bound would be an advantage.
- Wish to work through every weekend and cancel all your holidays.

This is an exciting opportunity to become totally involved in one of the most forward-thinking companies in the whole world.

If people like this existed, would you really need a Channel Partner?

They do exist. They are our Channel Partners. They don't just sell IT products. They provide you with independent, impartial advice and only supply Compaq products as part of complete IT solutions. First they listen and learn about your business, then they predict your IT needs so your systems grow with you. Expensive expertise? Not when they lower your cost of ownership. Can you afford not to use them? Call your Computacenter Account Manager or call Computacenter direct on 0800 617 000.

COMPAQ NonStop™

Chapter 6

Using technology to manage information

Carl Taylor and Richard Harvey, both e-business architects at The iGroup, the eBusiness division of Computacenter, emphasise the crucial role that technology has to play in helping an organisation reach its knowledge management goals

Information technology provides the means of capturing, storing and retrieving the data and information sources that form the basis of "knowledge" and is a fundamental component of any successful knowledge management strategy.

Knowledge management technologies spring from two main sources: the universal communications medium of the internet and established technology, such as information retrieval, document management and workflow processing tools. By facilitating quicker and better-informed decision making, these technologies make processes more efficient and effective – and often substantially cheaper. Most of the information that people need for planning and decision-making is already present somewhere in the organisation. The problem is that an organisation does not always know what information it has, or where to find it.

KNOWING WHAT YOU KNOW

The problem of accessing and benefiting from tacit knowledge cannot be solved by the simple application of standard technology tools. Over 80 per cent of corporate information resides as data that is both unstructured and unmanaged. This defies a neatly packaged IT solution and instead requires a broader methodology.

Like any other business project, knowledge management is most successful when the organisation takes a benefits-driven approach and starts by defining the desired results, rather than concentrating on the knowledge itself.

Taking an information intranet as a potential platform for knowledge management, a company should carry out the following process to determine whether this technology will address its objectives:

1. *Start by looking at the business's problems and processes, and identifying where and whether an information intranet will help with them;*

2. *Next, user profiling should be employed to determine what information is important to people working on these cycles, by finding out which documents they view as being key;*

3. *Finally, establish the business justification for better provision of information, such as aiming for a faster sales cycle or quicker product development.*

This strategic business approach lies at the heart of successful knowledge management. And with the help of these analyses, it is possible to build systems that will benefit the people working on the key business cycles, and provide the necessary information for faster and better-informed decision-making.

CREATING THE DEMAND FOR KNOWLEDGE

Essentially, knowledge sharing will only be successful when a market for knowledge is created. This means that there needs to be both supply and demand. Eventually, the shared knowledge base will lead to the erosion of private power bases, as more and more high-quality information becomes widely available online.

In this context, technology is an enabler, not a driver. That said, some solutions, when well implemented, can strongly influence organisational culture and help to bring about the necessary changes. In particular, if a technology solution provides quality information in a shared knowledge base that is fast and easy to access, it will stimulate greater demand for information and people will be encouraged to participate.

THE KNOWLEDGE MANAGEMENT PLATFORM

The requirements of knowledge management have inspired a range of new technologies in order to capture and share tacit knowledge that was previously out of reach. These technology enablers include:

■ *Directory services;*

■ *Collaboration and messaging products;*

■ *Knowledge capture capability;*

■ *Analyses tools;*

■ *Search engines;*

■ *Delivery and tracking tools.*

Depending on the organisation's needs, these are used in varying combinations to form a knowledge management platform.

Directory services

Directory services are fast becoming a core component of an organisation's technical infrastructure. In the context of knowledge management, a directory service is a function that enables user profiles to be stored. These profiles range from formal structured information, such as contact details and job titles, to informal unstructured information such as interests and hobbies. This information is accessbile to all knowledge management applications within the organisation.

Collaboration and messaging

Messaging is one of the most important of the knowledge management technologies. It allows people to collaborate easily and communicate and make decisions quickly. It is also the element of the knowledge management platform that is widely available today through e-mail systems such as Microsoft Exchange or Lotus Notes.

As well as the core messaging these products also offer shared documents, calendars and tasks to create rich collaborative environments within the organisation.

Capture and business vocabulary

The effective capture of information by individuals is a key element of managing knowledge. Only when this process is properly managed can it be mobilised across the organisation to the benefit of all. To do this effectively information flows need to be analysed and tagged against a business vocabulary, allowing it to be consistently indexed and retrieved in the appropriate context. This vocabulary is a defined list of shared terms that describe the information sources that the business uses. It is constructed by a process of information analysis that is widely referred to as the practice of "information architecture."

It is only by employing such a vocabulary that information can be effectively shared within the organisation using technology. For example, consider the situation where departments use alternative terms for the same product; it is only when these terms are rationalised that information can be easily shared in a common system such as an intranet (see case study on page 47).

Analysis of data

Typically, businesses use analysis tools to learn more about what they and their competitors are doing performing "what if" scenarios that can help them improve their understanding and anticipate business trends. This analysis, in turn, can lead to better business planning decisions.

In the past, one of the central problems facing effective analysis was the inability to combine data sources from disparate back-end systems in a meaningful way, so that its value as knowledge could be released. Fortunately, software producers have now created analysis products that allow non-technical users to visualise and easily manipulate data, such as the existing sales of products, to identify business trends and aid decision-making.

Search and search engines

Search facilities are a prerequisite of an efficient and successful knowledge management platform. They can, for instance, enable a person to find an expert in a given area or a document to help with a specific business problem.

Please arrange for Computacenter to telephone me to discuss my knowledge management requirements

Please send me further information on Computacenter's e-business services

Please tick box

☐

☐

Name: _____

Title: _____

Company: _____

Address: _____

_____

Telephone: _____ E-mail: _____

Nature of business: _____

Number of computers in organisation:

| 1-50 ☐ | 51-100 ☐ | 101-300 ☐ |
| 301-500 ☐ | 501-1000 ☐ | Over 1000 ☐ |

NUSREEN ASKARI
THE IGROUP
COMPUTACENTER HOUSE
93-101 BLACKFRIARS ROAD
LONDON SE1 8YX

However, to make this process effective it is important that the search facility can index and retrieve the content of information sources and the business vocabulary that has been applied to it. The search engine then becomes a "context-based" system that can cater for both general user queries and pre-defined searches and automatically create links between related content and users.

Delivery

Companies rely on the right information being delivered to the right person, at the right time, ie. notifying relevant people when new marketing material about a product has been produced. The technology that facilitates this process includes user profiling within a directory service, which gives the user a degree of ownership of the content they want delivered. Content for delivery is usually identified using the search facility and relies heavily on the business vocabulary discussed earlier.

Tracking

Technology can also help an organisation to measure the relevance and cost of its knowledge. This can be achieved by using automatic feedback loops – such as the number of times a document has been used – to measure the timeliness, accuracy and relevance of the information deployed.

Where a directory service and business vocabulary are being used the potential value of tracking is enhanced, especially when combined with user profiles and situational contexts. This can measure the relevance of the knowledge in a specific context, resulting in the information being delivered to other users with similar profiles or highlighted within a user search.

It is not often appreciated that the value of pieces of information within an organisation depreciates over time. Tracking may be used to identify this element of depreciation and ensure that information is either re-used to generate new knowledge or is archived to a content store. A typical example is the automation of information expiry on an intranet, by assigning expiry dates and "owners" to information at the time of capture. In this way, when information expires it may either be re-published or archived.

THE KNOWLEDGE MANAGEMENT PLATFORM IN PRACTICE

How does this work in practice? Take the following example of the way employee development could be managed by using the technologies outlined above:

■ *A user directory service would be used to store employee contact details and to index the skills (taken from the business vocabulary) that each employee holds.*

■ *The training department would capture, and tag details of future events and distance learning materials, against skills, best practice guidelines, etc. to form a content store.*

■ *Collaboration features would be used to maintain calendars of events, training department contact details, and discussion forums for each of the skills.*

■ *The search engine would index this information and user profiles, enabling users to search for skills they want to acquire and be presented with relevant documents and links to people who already possess the skill and may serve as a mentor.*

■ *At this point a feedback loop would be put in place to track that the user is interested in the skill and would update the user's entry in the directory service, as well as recording information usage and rate the usefulness of each piece of information they consume.*

■ *As new information is captured it could be automatically delivered to relevant users.*

■ *The training department could collect tracking data and analyse this against information held in the directory service to identify usage patterns and information areas that need re-evaluation.*

Today's technologies are giving organisations the ability to manage information effectively to create knowledge. However, it is only by combining these technologies in a holistic platform that an organisation will derive the most benefit from a knowledge management strategy.

It is important to stress that knowledge management solutions create new challenges not previously encountered with more demanding traditional IT systems; they require an unprecedented level of organisational integration to be truly successful. Fundamentally, knowledge management is about using technology to manage data and information to create knowledge, and integrating this with the company's people and culture.

COMPANY-WIDE COMMUNICATIONS

When Napp Pharmaceuticals, a world leader in manufacturing, drug discovery, development and manufacture of prescription drugs, wanted to capture its entire intellectual capital and making it easily accessible to staff via the company's intranet, it called on Computacenter's iGroup to find and implement a solution

This ongoing project began two years ago when Napp called in The iGroup to help construct the company's intranet site. This was developed to maintain user skills and facilitate an understanding of intranet/internet technologies, including "live" video, weekend weather, social event information, a canteen/restaurant menu and daily news feeds.

While very successful, the site was not easily scalable and Napp lacked the in-house resources to keep it up to date. As a result, Phase II was to focus on finding an alternative way of structuring the intranet that would widen publishing opportunities and transfer the responsibility for keeping content up to date to the individual departments.

The iGroup presented Napp with an intranet management system that uses a combination of HTML and MetaTag technologies. The iFramework allows a company to store any type of document, including text, graphics, sound and video from originals created in formats as diverse as Microsoft Office, JPEG graphics and Quicktime movie clips, and carry out sophisticated searches using simple English.

However, in order for the system to work properly, you have to start with a common business vocabulary and define an information architecture to ensure that all documents are properly identified to the intranet. The first part of the challenge was already well underway. Napp had developed a business thesaurus of its most commonly used terms and descriptions.

However, the information architecture was an area where it felt it could benefit from outside input. Sean Warren, Napp's Intranet Project Manager, explains: "Different people have different perceptions of the same thing. For example, a salesman's view of a report is a very much less detailed document than a research chemist's.

We also found that there are many words that we spell differently around the company, even though English is our common language."

"We set out to analyse and identify all the different types of document created by the company and develop a common architecture and vocabulary for their description. The iGroup's information architecture model enables us to map out our intranet content. We grouped documents by the way they will be used, the departments or activities to which they relate and their nature and identified 43 different categories of information."One unexpected benefit of the exercise was that it revealed a large number of duplicate documents, either due to earlier versions not having been cleared, or because there were slightly different emphases for different audiences. The decision to publish a single document whenever possible is expected to lead to a significant reduction in the overall document volume.

The information architecture also created the means to tighten up version control substantially. It proposed that all master documents to be held on the server, allowing version control to be maintained strictly, and has given responsibility for updating or deleting the document to its original author.

The development of such an effective model will mean that all users become empowered to publish information, and will be able to do so using their existing desktop software. Because The iFramework retrieves documents from the intranet and displays them in a web browser, users do not need to learn the intricacies of HTML layouts and can publish freely. The iFramework also manages the update process, returning documents to authors for a decision to update or delete as appropriate.

One caveat on which Sean Warren insists is that when people first save documents they are required to complete a summary page that describes the document type and content, and append a set of keywords that relate to it for use by the search engine. Authors can also define who should have access to the document, either as a public domain document, restricted to themselves, or by nominated individuals or group.

The final development of the information architecture is Napp's People-to-People database. This uses information stored on every staff member's home page, combined with their bibliography of publications, to help colleagues contact other members of the company who may be able to contribute to their projects.

Chapter 7

A practical insight

In an increasingly competitive climate, companies cannot afford to ignore the demands of the knowledge-based business. Nick Langley, business and IT writer, explores the issue of organisations using knowledge as a product

Retailers and the like have long realised the value in harvesting knowledge from their customers: what they buy, when they buy and how they buy. These are the sorts of gems of knowledge they can use to fine-tune their sales and marketing strategies.

However, it is only recently that the concept of using web-based technologies to manage knowledge as a sellable "product" has been actively employed by corporates.

Take Amazon.com, for instance. Since launching, the well-known Seattle-based internet bookseller has traded on the basis of disseminating database-driven information and knowledge about books – descriptions of content, synopses and customer reviews – to its customers. Then by seamlessly automating the ordering process and providing excellent customer support, it uses the requests from its customer base – now over 10 million - to analyse customer preferences to achieve re-sales. Amazon.com, therefore, is not so much in the business of selling books (which, of course, it does as an end product), but knowledge about books to achieve commercial success. Arguably, therefore, Amazon's whole success is built on selling knowledge as a product.

Cost efficiency comes from understanding the customers' needs through the knowledge gained, and then implementing best practices to streamline the technology and operations. Interestingly, the same pieces of knowledge become important for e-business as for e-commerce: What do our "customers" buy? When do they buy? And, how do they buy?

The typical corporate organisation makes hundreds of purchases a week – this represents a huge amount of purchasing data and trends (ie. knowledge) that remains untapped in most companies. The reason that this mine of information remains difficult to use is that internal service and product requistion is typically haphazard. Staff will raise requisitions from a wide number of suppliers (both internal and external). Frequently there is no one computer system that holds all of the requisition information and often processes are paper-based.

One organisation has addressed this by the introduction of a web-enabled e-procurement system. Computacenter's On-Trac electronic procurement system was designed nine years ago as an electronic price list to keep customers abreast of the rapid price changes, product introductions and discontinuations that characterise the IT industry. Customers wanted a tool on their desks that they could access for price and order details whenever they wanted. On-Trac combines "push" and "pull" technologies – that is, customers can dial out to it whenever they need information, but it is also regularly updated.

The application rapidly grew to include quotations, availability data and order placement. Customers see a customised list, showing only the products their organisation has standardised on, out of the 60,000 Computacenter provides. They also see the agreed price. Choosing the products automatically generates the quotation, and once approved, the quotation can be turned into a purchase order, which is automatically posted into a logistics engine. The order is then picked out of the warehouse and shipped the next day.

WIDENING THE NET

On-Trac has continued to grow in functionality, led by customers' wishes. Once installed at the customer's site, On-Trac can also be used to manage non-IT purchases from other suppliers – for example, mobile phones or office furniture. In some organisations, use of On-Trac has been extended to end users.

On-Trac can also be used to requisition internal services. As well as the laptop PC and mobile phone a new employee might need, On-Trac can, for example, requisition an intranet connection, Internet ID, business cards and a security pass.

By using the knowledge built up on each organisation's preferred suppliers and corporate technology standards in this way, On-Trac lowers the cost of raising the requisition for the customer. It also lowers the cost of sale, which can be passed on to the customer. It makes sales and sales support people more proactive, and has led to a big reduction in returns and errors. Customers can track the progress of their order without having to ring the supplier. Rules can be drawn up to define what products and pricing the customer sees, either by the supplier's account managers, or by the customers IT department.

PUTTING THE PLAN INTO ACTION

Reed Business Information (RBI), the fourth largest of the Reed Elsevier companies, uses On-Trac. "We have recently set up Service Level Agreements with the business, which include a guaranteed time from placement of an order to implementation," says Neil Argent, head of Business Systems Support at RBI, which has also set up a series of defined hardware standards. All the pre-defined product sets are entered into the system to simplify users' options and reduce the chance of user error.

When a user requests a new system, they are visited by a support team member to assess their needs. This information is entered into On-Trac, which immediately creates a quote based on current prices. This is forwarded to the relevant cost centre manager and finance department for sign-off, and then back to the support team where On-Trac manages the final sign-off process electronically. With a couple of key strokes, the administrative team turns the approved quote into an order. At this point, the user is contacted and a date agreed for implementation.

"We can track orders quickly and easily," says Argent. "This has saved so much time that we used to spend chasing people. We used to make a lot of mistakes with our manual process: we were recreating the wheel every time we placed an order. When a network card was missed off or the wrong memory specified, we ended up with additional delays to the process." With the On-Trac system, if an order has to be amended prior to send-off, it can be electronically sent back for further amendment.

Reed uses On-Trac to highlight quotes that have been outstanding for over a month and not turned into orders. Follow-up calls can either speed up the process, or cancel a system that is no longer required. The introduction of this system has also significantly reduced administration work. Since the instigation of the Computacenter relationship, the company has embarked on a roll-out of millennium-compliant systems, significantly increasing the volumes of orders. Argent says they are ordering an average of 60 new machines a month.

"Without access to On-Trac we would have had to increase the number of staff handling new system procurement and implementation," he says. The company is also exploiting the statistical and management information delivered by Computacenter. This has already highlighted some potential savings, including moving from daily to twice-weekly deliveries. "Detailed information on the sales of each model every month is being used by the directors to assess the effectiveness of our IT spend," Argent explains.

Linklaters is an international legal practice operating from the UK and other major financial centres. Its customers are multinational corporations, global investment banks, financial institutions and national governments. Documents are the firm's key business output, so document management has become the firm's most business-critical application. Of the million or so documents produced each year, many are shared or jointly authored by teams located across the world. Linklaters installed Documentum's enterprise document management system so that it could make any document available to any authorised individual in the company at any time, anywhere in the world. Currently all 2,400 Linklaters' staff and over 350 active concurrent users can access one central document base.

"It gives us a core reusable knowledge infrastructure," says Simon Thompson, Linklaters' Head of Information Systems. The system, which is fully integrated with Microsoft Office, facilitates knowledge management and Intranet management and delivery, as well as providing a transaction index.

Working with Documentum, Linklaters has created a new legal documentation offering as part of its Blue Flag suite of products. "Legal services revolve around advice and counselling, documentation, and transaction management," says Mark Boggis, Linklaters' Blue Flag business manager. "Our clients demand 100 per cent accuracy and judgment, continuous availability and responsiveness."

Blue Flag replaces the conventional customised legal delivery mechanism with an electronically enabled, commoditised one, addressing essential legal issues. The newest service, Blue Flag confirms, is tailored for investment banks. It automatically completes confirmations of trades in the Over the Counter (OTC) derivatives market by taking data generated by the trader, and incorporating it automatically in the confirmation. Where legal input is required, Blue Flag Confirms analyses the requirement and selects the appropriate term or definition. The output is then customised to reflect the user's own preferences, from preferred legal terminology down to the typeface of the document.

INTEGRATED KNOWLEDGE MANAGEMENT

Until now, knowledge management solutions have required a number of technologies to be integrated by consultants or user organisations themselves. "We will see the emergence of more integrated knowledge management offerings from vendors, who will need to expand the scope of their products," says Ovum's Woods. "We will see more amalgamation of the information retrieval and document management market."

Systems integrators and large management consultancies have been the most important force in the development of knowledge management and will continue to hold the largest part of this market. "Most management consultancies have knowledge management practices in place, and see immense opportunities for expansion in coming years, both in helping organisations to understand their knowledge management needs at business level, and as systems integrators, pulling together different technologies," says Woods.

HEWLET
PACKARD

hot, true

or mellow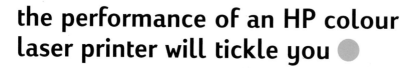

the performance of an HP colour laser printer will tickle you

Nothing adds impact to your business documents like colour. It increases comprehension by up to 73%, improves readership by up to 40% and accelerates learning by up to 78%.

And whatever size your business or workgroup is, HP's Color LaserJet printers will give you professional colour that's fast, reliable and affordable. With HP's leading-edge technology such as HP PhotoREt II and HP ColorSmart, the HP range passes with flying

HP Color LaserJet 4500

Exceptional, A4 colour laser printing for workgroups of 5-10 people.

- 4 pages per minute in colour and 16 in mono
- 600-dpi with HP Image REt 2400
- Network compatible
- Automatic duplexing option
- Prints on heavy media up to 135g/m²

HP Color LaserJet 8500

The departmental laser printer for all your A4 and A3 colour printing.

- Automatic duplexing option
- 6 pages per minute in colour and 24 in mono
- 600-dpi with HP Image REt 2400
- Network compatible
- Prints on heavy media up to 216g/m²

So use your ● matter.

For more information on HP's Color LaserJet printers

Call 0870 606 47 47 quoting ref. 10D/12/99

Chapter 8

Memory-making for innovation

Alan Malachowski, business writer, explains how companies can maintain continuity of knowledge without becoming overburdened by their past

Back in the forties, the economist and political theorist F A Hayek argued that "the economic problem of society is not merely a problem of how to allocate resources...it is a problem of utilisation of knowledge". Following Hayek, we can think of companies as complex cognitive systems whose well-being depends on a capacity to acquire, process and retain knowledge. And, we can think of this knowledge as "information" about products and/or services which is mediated by the market.

THE TURNOVER TENDENCY

In fast-moving, competitive economies, information that has no immediate connection to the marketplace is considered redundant. For the emphasis has shifted to "knowledge turnover" – its acquisition and processing rather than its retention. Modern management techniques serve a diuretic function in this respect. They flush out stale knowledge to make way for fresh, market-sensitive input. Only a company which is fast on its informational feet can sustain the level of innovation required for commercial success these days. Or so it seems.

ORGANISATIONAL AMNESIA

Business is afraid of being overwhelmed by its past. However, a company which is unable to retain knowledge and lives only for the "informational moment", may be unwittingly compelled to relive its past.

Consider a familiar scenario: A company relocates a significant proportion of its core business operations. This decision imposes costs, both financial and social. But the benefits are estimated to outweigh such costs. Then, ten years later, the company decides to bring most of the very same operations within one premises. Again, the decision generates costs. But, once more, the predicted benefits appear to justify the decision. Five years on, having been correct in its cost calculations, the company continues to flourish.

Now imagine the same situation occurring when the company in question possesses very little "organisational memory". What is likely to happen to the cost calculations? Clearly they are likely to fail, and badly. For in such circumstances:

- *The initial decision to relocate may be made in ignorance of the costs of past performances in that sphere (what if the company had already been through a cycle of sending out related operations and then bringing them back in?).*

- *The second decision to bring things back in-house is liable to take place behind a further veil of ignorance regarding the relocated business area it seeks to reverse.*

Since what has been described here could also happen with "re-engineering", "downsizing" and so on, it is not difficult to imagine the havoc organisational amnesia can wreck in terms of human resources as well as bottom line, financial costs.

HOW SYSTEMATIC FORGETFULNESS GETS A GRIP

Organisational memory has two main components: human and technological. Both are necessary, and each can serve as a useful check on the other.

The human side of "memory" may begin to deteriorate when staff-turnover accelerates. Things can then reach a point where there is no one around who remembers the trials and tribulations of previous projects. As for the technological component, this may start to become less effective when strategy outstrips both corporate reporting and the hard data preserved about past performance.

When a company loses sight of its own history, its record of successes and failures, then its very identity is threatened. From an insider's point of view, the workplace environment will be frustrating – one in which timely advice is scarce and even minor decisions are liable to come unstuck. And, from an external perspective, such as that of a potential investor, the company will appear to have no strategic sense of direction. A company devoid of adequate memory resources will tend to thrash around in the market place like a rudderless ship at sea.

MEMORY-MAKING: PREVENTION AND CURE

As Dorothy Leonard and Susan Straus point out in their Harvard Business Review article of July/August 1997, *Putting your Company's Whole Brain to Work*, "innovate or fall behind" is "the creative imperative for virtually all business today". However, innovative success does not strike companies like a bolt out of the blue. Instead, it emerges from what management guru Peter Drucker calls "a commitment to the systematic practice of innovation". This "systematic practice", or "discipline of innovation", as Drucker also puts it, requires the springboard of organisational support. And a vital element of such support has to come in the shape of memory-based knowledge management.

How can a company ensure that its memory does not become prematurely impaired? How can it avoid the organisational equivalent of Alzheimer's disease?

In less frenetic times, the human side of organisational memory was able to evolve gradually over time through customs, rituals and repetitive workplace practices. Companies were able to weave a narrative around their exploits which enchanted employee and investor alike.

By contrast, in today's commercial environment, businesses do not have the luxury of being able to wait for the social aspects of their memory functions to fall naturally into place. The challenge now is to consciously foster and develop what used to be the product of a long line of unconscious processes. In short, companies need to experiment in order to find the practical methods of memory-making which suit their commercial needs.

Such "methods" may include the introduction of information-sharing gatherings (both formal and informal), interactive newsletters and retrospective celebrations (where the company collectively looks back over its past achievements).

Companies can also investigate the ways in which the deployment of physical space within the business premises influences the flow of information. Do the people who have specific knowledge of key projects get a chance to meet and chat on a regular basis? Does the layout of the building create distinct repositories of knowledge? If so, can these be dipped into by employees who occupy another part of the building?

While the methodology of memory-making ought to be highly customised, the overall aims should be the same in every case:

- *To inspire employees to take a keen interest in the details of their company's commercial activities;*

- *To encourage information-sharing in forms which reinforce the company's ongoing sense of its commercial identity;*

- *To facilitate a high degree of personal awareness concerning "information responsibilities" (so that everyone is clear about who can be relied on for information).*

TECHNOLOGY – THE HUMAN TOUCH

In the current turmoil of "restructuring", companies have become obsessed with change for change's sake, as if only a process of continually re-inventing themselves can ward off premature extinction. Before this obsession turns into a destructive addiction, business needs to start asking serious questions about the human consequences of its proposed changes. And, such questions must cater for the ways in which human activity gains much of its signifance from the historical context within which it occurs.

As Hamel and Prahalad point out in their bestselling book *Competing For The Future*, "Creating the future doesn't require a company to abandon all its past. Indeed, a critical question for every firm is: What part of our past can we use as a "pivot" to get to the future, and what part of our past represents excess baggage?".

The construction of an appropriately-managed knowledge culture is made less daunting by the sheer wealth and versatility of the available technological resources. To a certain extent, these resources make up for a shortfall on the culture side (eg. if people are unable to meet face to face, they can communicate by e-mail). But brute technology should not be allowed to become a substitute for the personal dimension of knowledge-retention.

All companies need to heed the advice given on information technology resources throughout this guide. By building up a suitable database, together with flexible, company-wide modes of access and interaction, a company can install a memory-generating framework which is to a significant degree self-managing. But, at some stage in interpretation and implementation, data needs the human touch.

With a technologically sophisticated, memory-making framework in place and informational-aware, human hands on the tiller, a company should be able to navigate the unchartered waters of innovation without leaving behind the commercial landmarks of its previous journeys.

Chapter 9

Benchmarking your success

Knowledge management is a continuous process. Having implemented a new strategy, what techniques can companies employ to measure whether or not their strategy is working? Carol Kennedy, business writer, investigates

Lew Platt, the former chief executive of Hewlett Packard, once memorably defined the whole purpose of knowledge management in a sentence: "If HP knew what HP knows, it would be three times as profitable."

Most organisations, of whatever size and in whatever industry, have a huge hidden asset that could be making profits but daily goes to waste for lack of knowing what the asset consists of, where it is lurking within the organisation and how to manage and leverage it for improved performance. That asset consists of the knowledge and experience of the business accumulated by its employees over time and practice; knowledge of customers, competitors, suppliers, processes, research, costs, marketing opportunities, past mistakes – the list is endless.

Intellectual capital is no mere figure of speech, as can be seen in the huge differences between the stockmarket valuation and net book value of leading knowledge-intensive companies. Microsoft is the prime example, a company whose capital assets are minuscule compared to the value the market places on its capacity to innovate and lead a global industry. Amazon.com is an even more astonishing phenomenon, a company built on an idea, where knowledge management is literally its product. It has an enormous market capitalisation but has yet to turn a profit.

A study of the ratio between tangible and intangible assets in different industries, carried out by the Gartner Group in 1998, showed health and personal care at the top, with stockmarket valuation nearly four times book value. (Knowledge management is of prime importance in the pharmaceutical industry because so much of its new product development springs from past knowledge.) Beverages and tobacco, where the intangible value lies mostly in brand image and market position, came second in the Gartner ranking, followed by broadcasting and publication.

Even an apparent smokestack industry such as steel could muster stockmarket valuations of two-and-a-half times book value. The shift in the ratio of intangible to tangible assets will increase across all industries, the study concluded, especially among the high-tech sectors and many service industries.

CAPITALISING ON INTANGIBLE ASSETS

As yet, comparatively few companies have made the connection between this phenomenon and capitalising on their intangible assets. However, research organisations involved with knowledge management, however, expect its future growth to be very rapid. A survey by the Delphi Group in 1998 found that nearly 30 per cent of their respondents had already adopted a knowledge management programme. More than half expected to do so within one year and 95.7 per cent believed they would within four years. Financial services are well ahead of the field, followed by chemicals and plastics, technology, and then telecommunications and pharmaceuticals.

As techniques evolve for measuring results in knowledge management and – more persuasively for the bean-counters – for measuring the return on investment in the technology, even this rate could be surpassed. So how does a company go about finding out "what it knows?"

Some of the knowledge and experience within it (the least important and the easiest to retrieve) will be in the form of data. The next level up is information, or key data that has been analysed and meaningfully interpreted, and the third is explicit or transferable knowledge. The two top levels are both the most valuable and the most difficult to extract: tacit knowledge, which is held in the heads of individuals, and finally, the synthesis at the top – more commonly called "wisdom."

Knowledge management is essentially about converting tacit knowledge into explicit knowledge that can be shared throughout the organisation. No part of the conversion process, indeed no effective knowledge management at all, would be possible without the enabling power of technology – basically, systems such as groupware and intranets – and this is where benchmarking emerges as a key tool. Given that the object of any effective knowledge management programme is to get the right information to the right person at the right time, benchmarking must begin internally by first establishing where and why knowledge management will deliver its best value and where it will make the most difference, whether by saving costs, cutting cycle times or some other competitive advantage.

CRUCIAL QUESTIONS FOR BENCHMARKING

All benchmarking techniques begin with three questions, says Professor Tony Bendell of the University of Leicester, a leading national authority on the subject: where do we want to be, where are we now, and what do we need to do to get from here to there? The answers to these will be different for each company. This is why external benchmarking against competitors, normal practice in other areas of business, is less effective in knowledge management.

As Mark Auckland, head of knowledge management at BT, points out, it depends on your business and market and what you want knowledge management to do – codification of knowledge and its re-use, knowledge creation, or the type of intellectual capital valuation pioneered by Skandia, the Swedish financial services group, for example. There are good benchmark models but "no one best way," says Auckland. He has built up his own dossier of companies whose knowledge management practices have impressed him. They include Nokia, ABB, Shell and BP, but he emphasises that it is an informal process.

Some ready-made external benchmarking, which may offer useful pointers, is provided in *The Most Admired Knowledge*

Enterprises Report, published by Management Trends International. This used a set of eight key performance drivers to identify 20 companies as world-class in knowledge management, topped by Lucent Technologies, the former AT&T spin-off. The report includes case studies on all 20 companies, drawing best practice lessons from each. The drivers were:

- *Overall quality of knowledge programme;*

- *Top management support;*

- *Contribution to innovation;*

- *Maximising intellectual assets;*

- *Effectiveness of knowledge sharing;*

- *Culture of continuous learning;*

- *Creating customer value and loyalty;*

- *Contribution to shareholder value.*

In general, internal benchmarking should be both qualitative (gained through surveys and interviews) and quantitative (through such raw data as the number of meetings held, e-mails received, calls made to a help line). To quantify progress made each of these inquiries can be repeated after the knowledge management system has been operating for a given period. Both types of measurement can be further refined in a matrix to determine the success of the knowledge management system, and the time saved for each person can be measured in terms of salaries to achieve a real ROI.

SELF-ASSESSMENT TOOLKIT

A useful self-assessment toolkit for auditing your company's "knowledge culture" is provided in a report by the Kent-based research institute Create. The report, *Good Practices in Knowledge Creation and Exchange*, stresses that technology alone – while indispensable in enabling a company to communicate and share findings within itself and, in global operations, across geographic areas in real time – will not work without a culture of understanding human relationships and motivation. "Converting tacit knowledge into explicit knowledge is more about business cultures than physical structures," say authors Professor Amin Rajan and Kirsty Chapple and ICL's Elizabeth Lank.

Put bluntly, in an age of downsizing people want to know why they should disburse valuable knowledge which could give them a professional advantage. Companies with successful knowledge management programmes recognise this and build in incentives. Motorola, for example, assures employees that they will not lose out if they share knowledge of their mistakes as well as successes.

The toolkit comprises a series of scored questions that audits the state of the company's systems, values and behaviours by asking how relevant each factor listed is to the organisation's current circumstances, and to what extent each is being implemented in the organisation. The score for relevance is then deducted from the implementation score and areas where the net score is negative are identified as those due for action.

FIVE KEY INNOVATIONS

Rajan and Chapple have further identified five key innovations that successful knowledge management companies such as AT&T, Fiat, Shell, BT and BP Amoco have implemented to overcome people's natural resistance to knowledge sharing. In the journal *Risk and Continuity* (March 1999) they listed these as:

- *An intelligent search engine in six sequential steps, starting with the installation of groupware or an intranet and the compilation of "yellow pages" listing individuals with special expertise in the organisation along with people who can act as "knowledge co-ordinators."*

- *Establishing communities of practice among peers "with a common sense of purpose and a real need to know what others know." These can tap corporate brainpower in areas ranging from R&D to marketing. They use the search engine as much as inter-personal contacts.*

■ *Establishing "virtual teams" – individuals in different locations and time zones who can share information and work together in real time by video-conferencing and using groupware such as Lotus Notes. BP Amoco is a leader in this field.*

■ *Action learning, designed through inter-personal communication to develop skills such as systems thinking, common mental models and team/self learning. Shell and BT regard this as a critical technique.*

■ *Culture-based learning – adopting the ethos and practice of professional services firms that live by creating and selling knowledge – for example, Ernst & Young, Arthur Andersen, and legal firms. Such firms have built a culture over time in which knowledge sharing is second nature.*

Chapter 10

Protecting your intellectual property

PART ONE: PROTECTION METHODS

Intellectual property is the currency of the future. But, as Laurence J Cohen, head of Intellectual Property at Hammond Suddards explains, there are practical legal issues involved in valuing and protecting knowledge assets

If you know something that your competitor does not know, and you know how to use it, you are one step ahead of your competitor. If your competitor can be prevented from using it you are two steps ahead of them. If your competitor can be prevented from using it and he knows it you are three steps ahead. All three steps involve the protection of intellectual property rights.

TRADE SECRETS

Knowledge, whether commercial or technical, can be protected as confidential information or a trade secret, provided it is substantial, recorded and secret. Trivial trade secrets are not protected; substantial trade secrets are. They are protected against piracy, including cyber hackers. They are also protected against current and ex-employees using them or selling them to third parties. Clearly, however, this is subject to the owner of the trade secret taking reasonable steps to protect the information. There is no registration system for protecting trade secrets.

COPYRIGHT

There are other ways of protecting knowledge. Copyright is the protection against copying. A copyright owner has the sole right to copy or reproduce the work in any material form. Reproduction or substantial reproduction is therefore prohibited by copyright.

Recorded material is subject to copyright which protects the form of the knowledge or creativity. Written work, including computer software, is protected as literary copyright. A sound track, a TV or cable programme, a performance, a musical and artistic work, works of art, architecture, sculptures, photographs, films and all other kinds of recorded creativity are protected by copyright.

Copyright is a right which subsists. It does not need to be registered, at least within the EU. However, the subject of copyright has to be recorded in a tangible and permanent form. The problem with copyright, however, is that it only protects the form of knowledge. The form in which knowledge is recorded is infringed by reproduction or substantial reproduction by adaptation or translation. However, not all such acts are infringement. While the acts of reproduction and first issuing such reproductions to the public in the UK are direct infringements, secondary acts of dealing in such reproduced works are not infringements unless the alleged infringer knew, or had reason to believe, that the reproduction was an infringing copy.

Quasi copyright – called design right – also protects designs. These are protected irrespective of aesthetic quality and protect engineering designs of all kinds.

The copyright protection period for literary, artistic or musical copyright and copyright in films is generally the life of the author, plus 70 years in most instances. The design right period is 15 years from the original design or 10 years from the first marketing. Licenses of right are available in the last five years of the design right. The class of persons entitled to unregistered design protection is very narrow, being citizens of the UK or the EEA and certain British colonies. In particular, designs made and first put on the market in the US or Japan are not normally protected by design right.

PROTECTING IDEAS

So the real problem concerns the protection of ideas. Where the idea can be kept confidential, it may be properly protected as a trade secret. But that does not stop others arriving independently at the same end point. Trade secrets are simply not viable where the very subject matter must be disclosed, such as a product, a book, a television programme or even an insurance policy.

PATENTING

The final means by which an idea can be protected is through the patent system, which is expensive. The Faustian bargain is that in return for disclosing your idea to the public, each country may grant you a limited monopoly of up to 20 years as having the sole right to put the idea into practice.

Since the cost of patenting is high – say £50,000 for one invention worldwide – many smaller companies do not bother. This is often short sighted. Patents can be exploited, so that even if a company does not have the means to exploit its knowledge, it can license it. This applies as much to patents as it does to copyright, and trade secrets. But the real money for manufacturing industry is in the area of patents, as they are visible. Trade secrets and copyright are valuable too, especially where there is a process which cannot be replicated, or the subject matter is artistically creative, such as in the music and film industry.

THE DANGER OF KEEPING KNOWLEDGE TO YOURSELF

Whether to use licensing to exploit knowledge which you cannot sensibly exploit yourself can be a difficult call. You could keep the knowledge to yourself. Awards for damages for patent infringement in the US have exceeded $100m on a number of occasions.

In the case of Kodak v Polaroid in the early 1980s, the cost of damages paid to Polaroid came to almost $1bn, including interest. Despite the huge award, this case illustrates the danger of keeping technology to yourself through patents, when you really ought to be licensing. The award was Polaroid's swan song. Who today uses Polaroid colour film? The company kept the product to itself and killed the market because no one else was interested in it. One-hour processing, the good and cheap 35mm format, and now the digital camera, have led most customers to bypass Polaroid's instant film technology. There is a very real danger that unless you disseminate knowledge it will be superceded in this way.

No company has understood this better than Microsoft. Its knowledge is in operating systems. It also produces good applications software, which it packages well. It keeps its core knowledge to itself, but allows others to piggy-back onto that knowledge. Both sides benefit: other players can take advantage of Microsoft's knowledge, while it takes advantage of the knowledge of others to reinforce the need to buy its core products.

CONTRACTS

But knowledge cannot always be categorised neatly. Knowledge of how to do something may be personal. Some skills cannot be learnt. This kind of knowledge can be protected to limited extent by contract. In particular, contracts of employment in proper form, with valid restrictive covenants to prevent or limit post-termination competition, may be appropriate to lock in individuals with high knowledge.

This cannot be an absolute, but as a rule of thumb, the more valuable an individual and the more specialised his knowledge, the more likely a restrictive covenant is to be appropriate. And knowledge, like flavour, needs to be locked in at an early stage. It is no use trying to recapture knowledge that has flown. Contracts need to be in place at an early stage of employment.

Ultimately, knowledge which has flown, or rights which have been infringed, have to be protected through the courts. Each country, including each member state of the EEA, has its own legal system and courts. Pan European litigation is possible to a limited extent, but not currently in respect of registered rights such as patents and trademarks.

The enforcement process can be expensive, especially where the real argument is whether valid third-party rights have been infringed. This is usually where the arguments arise. Does the claimant have the scope of right he claims, and is he entitled to protect it across the whole scope of what he is claiming? Since commercial decisions are taken on assessment of that issue, litigation to protect knowledge against third party appropriation tends to be hard fought. Therefore, knowledge without the money to enforce and protect it is also not worthwhile.

These days the insurance industry is alive to the fact that we live in a knowledge-based economy and is prepared to protect against the misappropriation of that knowledge. Insurance companies will insure both against litigation expenses and against the diminution in value of an intellectual property portfolio.

The generation and exploitation of knowledge is nothing new. While news of the British victory at Waterloo in 1815 was available to everyone, the Rothschild banking family made arrangements to get the news privately and more quickly than anyone else. This enabled it to take the appropriate steps to deal with the consequences. This was public knowledge used by them faster and to better effect than anyone else.

The same is true of the internet. The medium is available to all, yet only a few can exploit it. How to exploit an opportunity is knowledge of the highest order, in which a traditional intellectual property analysis has no place. Knowledge and intellectual property protection overlap, but are not synonymous. Smart planning and good advice are essential.

PART TWO: TECHNICAL ISSUES

Charles Brown, consultant, outlines the particular set of challenges and opportunities presented by digital technologies for owners of intellectual property

The capability of digital technologies to make perfect copies of an original digital work, and the existence of increasingly ubiquitous electronic networks, which allow the distribution of copies at little or no cost, simultaneously raises the spectre of massive piracy and opens up enormously attractive commercial possibilities.

In addition to these characteristics, digital networks and

formats allow content to be divided into smaller units than would be economically viable using analogue technologies and physical distribution systems. A single newspaper or scientific journal article; a page or table from a report; an update to a textbook or operations manual; one music track – all these are now practical slices of content for digital distribution.

Alongside the more granular division of intellectual property goes the multiplicity of payment and use options that become possible as more and more users are connected to digital networks.

Pay-per-view films and events have been available for some years on analogue cable and satellite television systems in the US and Europe, so the principle of paying for a single "use" of a piece of content is nothing new. But the expansion of bandwidth available on digital systems and, crucially, the ability to handle any content that can be digitised, makes this principle extendable to text, audio, image and other types of video content.

Combined with new encryption technologies, it becomes possible to set rules under which particular pieces of content can be sold and used, and attach these rules to the content itself (see case study overleaf). Given the dangers of piracy inherent in digital formats, it is imperative that the rules and the content go together.

The capacity of digital content to contain embedded or attached rules of use allows further distributive twists. On the one hand, differential pricing can be attached to the same piece of content: the first use could cost more than repeat uses, for example. Another option would be to permit one-off screenings of a video to larger groups (eg. a Disney video to a children's party in advance of the normal availability) for a higher payment.

On the other hand, users can be permitted, or actively encouraged, to pass content on to other people who they think would also like to purchase it. This model is known as "superdistribution" or "viral marketing" – because the content spreads like a virus along multiple pathways which would probably be imperfectly reached by conventional marketing methods.

The changes that are possible in the production, marketing, sale and distribution of intellectual property as a result of the spread

Cranberry Grove was set up in October 1999 by The iGroup in partnership with NatWest Magex

Established to help music industry insiders explore secure digital music distribution, Cranberry Grove allows pilot members to engage with the business models and opportunities presented by the digital marketplace.

Until now, copyright theft has prevented owners of premium music making their content freely available on the Internet. The Cranberry Grove encryption software is designed to change this. Built around secure hosting services, digital rights management (DRM) technology from InterTrust Technologies Corp. and advanced payment clearance systems, it takes the risk out of putting quality content online. And this security has attracted some significant names. Among other leading players, Sanctuary Music Group, songs.com, Big Heavy World, and Tunes.com have all signed up to the pilot.

For the time being, Cranberry Grove – a free pilot built around the cranberrygrove.com website – is for music industry insiders only. And this is part of its appeal. Safe in the knowledge that their music is only available to a restricted audience, content owners can experiment without exposing themselves to the risk of copyright theft.

of digital technologies also bring with them major implications for:

- *Business models (eg. traditional bundles of content such as the academic journal, the newspaper and the music album may be disaggregated);*

- *Relationships between individual creators (writers, musicians, journalists and others) and traditional packagers and distributors;*

- *Relationships between consumers (whether personal or business) and the creators and owners of content;*

- *Consumer behaviour;*

- *The increasingly complex management of digital assets by content owners, who need to track smaller units of content across multiple platforms.*

The area of intellectual property that has been most dramatically affected by digital distribution so far has been music. Innovations in compressing the size of files – notably the MP3 format (short for Moving Pictures Experts Group or MPEG-1 Layer 3) – mean that music tracks can now be downloaded from the Internet on to PCs in a fraction of the time it used to take.

Consumer electronics companies have responded to the opportunity by creating portable MP3 devices, such as the Diamond Rio player. Web sites have sprung up to act as portals or aggregators of MP3 tracks. Alongside legitimate tracks that are sold online or given away for promotional purposes, mainly from new artists or independent labels, there are pirated MP3 files from established artists available on the Internet.

Chapter 11

Shaping the future

Rob Tarling and David Fletcher – respectively eBusiness Consultant and Head of Solutions at The iGroup of Computacenter – emphasise that the future belongs to those companies that are able to unlock the opportunities that knowledge management offers

If you want to understand the real potential of knowledge management one need look no further than Lara Croft – the cult heroine of the Tomb Raider computer game. Five years ago, Lara was nothing more than an itch at the back of someone's brain. Next she became a sketch on a piece of paper. Then she was turned into billions of digital signals in a computer. Now she sits at the very heart of Eidos's success, the company that created her and has subsequently seen its market value shoot up to over £1bn as a result.

Eidos's story demonstrates how in the knowledge economy business will be built on concepts that people have never thought of before. It puts a premium on imagination and innovation, and the ability to bring ideas to market fast.

However, imagination and innovation will not be the exclusive preserve of the newly emergent players of the knowledge economy. They are the key qualities that any company in any industry will need to compete and even survive going forward. Of course, there will be new businesses like Eidos, built upon previously undreamed of concepts. But there will also be many existing businesses in all kinds of industries that will reap a new lease of life by tapping the well of knowledge management.

ANY INDUSTRY CAN BENEFIT

Take financial services, for example, which is faced with unprecedented change as a result of the dual pressures of the knowledge economy and the new dictates of e-business (the two concepts are, of course, closely linked). In an ever accelerating cycle – itself a reflection of the changes now underway - the banking and insurance industries receive constantly changing information from many sources – whether it is the preferences of their customers or the competitive environment in which they operate.

Their challenge is to find ways to use and then react to this information to enable them to present a better value proposition to both customers and stakeholders - both of whom are increasingly savy about who to "trust" in the newly emergent economy. (One of the enduring features of the knowledge economy is that customers of organisations will be better informed, using the Internet to find perfect information about products and services.)

All of a sudden the investment that banks and building societies have made in national branch networks is beginning to look superfluous. As a result of changes in the way people communicate, new players are now emerging in financial services such as Prudential's Egg and retailers like Tesco that represent a fundamental challenge to the traditional players. To meet these challenges requires speed, agility and innovation – exactly the qualities that knowledge management seeks to foster.

Likewise, there are the global energy and petro-chemical industries, which with their massive investment in plant look unlikely candidates to benefit from the rise of the knowledge economy. But this is not necessarily so. Anything these companies can do to capture the knowledge invested in their existing programme, and then re-use it in others is likely to provide massive pay-offs. Take the case of BP Amoco. It estimates that it has saved more than £34m by transferring the knowledge it gained from its Andrew oil field in the North Sea to one of its new fields – Schiehallion.

The manufacturing sector also stands to gain from managing knowledge. Like the petro-chemical giants, it can win from systematising its knowledge from investments in new processes and machinery. But it can also make big gains from using knowledge about manufacturing processes to reduce errors and rejected batches. By cyclical learning about complex manufacturing processes wastage – and, therefore, total costs – are kept under

WORKING THE KNOWLEDGE MANAGEMENT WAY

The working environment of those companies that most successfully exploit the advantages of knowledge management will be very different from the traditional offices of the past

The once territorial hierarchy of individual offices is being replaced by a flexible space in which people can work and learn from one another in both formal and informal ways. Already, the leaders have started to experiment with new working environments for the knowledge economy.

One is British Airways with its new offices at Waterside, close to London's Heathrow airport. Instead of an office block, Waterside has been designed to operate more like a village community.

The surroundings are designed on an intimate human scale. There are covered thoroughfares which meander through the complex, with eating places and other meeting areas en route. The aim is to encourage people to wander, meet and chat. They can talk about the day's work and share their ideas. And technology is ever-present in an important supporting role – with PCs available to access information.

There are other ways in which Waterside reflects a typical knowledge management working space of the future. The complex operates a system of "hot desking" to encourage flexible working. Staff use laptop computers and book into working areas as they need them. Even Bob Ayling, the chief executive, makes do with a "space" rather than an office.

PowerGen is another company that is building more knowledge-focused working environments. Its headquarters near Coventry provides open and covered areas that offer more opportunities for chance encounters and includes communal spaces that can be used for informal meetings. There are cafe-style eating spaces to encourage social interaction.

tighter control. Once again, retailing is another industry that will increasingly use knowledge management to refine what it offers to customers. For example, some supermarkets are already able to vary the price of products according to the day of the week – and even the time of the day – depending on customer demand monitored by computer programs linked to point-of-sale terminals.

Retailers are also having to account for the growth of e-commerce via the internet and interactive TV. Whichever figures you choose to go with, it looks like the value of this market will be climbing on an exponential curve over the next few years. As this happens, retailers will need to learn more quickly about customer preferences in order to react to ever-changing demands.

Almost any company of any size is going to feel the impact of the knowledge economy, particularly as "digital convergence" pulls together the key elements that make knowledge management a reality rather than a myth.

DIGITAL CONVERGENCE AND MANAGING KNOWLEDGE

From examining trends it is possible to argue that three key elements are converging to enable genuine knowledge management within the corporate world.

The first of these – and most obvious to all – is the growing pervasiveness of the internet. By all measures this is the fastest growing communications medium in history, and this alone is driving the rapid development of technologies that seek to exploit this medium in this business world. As a result companies are increasingly finding that the use of internet – and, in particular, internet-protocol – technologies are becoming a "mission critical" part of their core technological infrastructure. This is providing the common platform on which a unified knowledge management strategy can be built.

The second is the growing recognition that knowledge management technologies - such as analysis, collaboration, messaging and information retrieval tools - are maturing to make it possible to effectively manage large amounts of information in increasingly diverse ways. Gartner Group, the IT research consultancy, estimates that we are now in a phase of consolidation of these technologies which within 3-5 years will genuinely enable the ultimate vision of knowledge management – that of serving information to the right person, at the right place at the right time.

Finally, attitudes within the business world are changing rapidly. While technology is a critical element of managing corporate know-how, it needs to be coupled with a genuine understanding of the role that knowledge can play in business. Senior executives need to grasp the strategic significance of knowledge management – both for their own companies and their industries as a whole. When the magazine *KMWorld* surveyed its readers in January 1999, more than two thirds picked out key strategic benefits such as improved decision-making, competitive advantage, the management of intellectual assets and increased innovation as being among the real pay-offs of knowledge management.

THE FUTURE

If only we knew what we know...in a sense this represents the key issue confronting managing knowledge in the Digital Age – if one were able to unlock the information and knowledge contained within corporate boundaries then the results could be truly dramatic. Now for the first time in history, internet technologies represent the chance to dramatically transform the way organisations handle the intellectual assets of their workers. Knowledge management is now moving beyond a management fad to a point where companies will use these technologies not only to seamlessly share information within their own workforce but also to tap into the immeasurable knowledge resources of the outside world.

Taking all this on board, the future for business in the knowledge economy may seem even more arcane than one of Lara Croft's adventures. But it need not be. Although knowledge management changes the rules of business, it does not invalidate the skills and experience that directors have acquired over the years. The winners in this new game will be those that interweave their own skills, experience and imagination with the new opportunities that knowledge management provides. For them, there really will be no boundaries to success.

For further information on managing knowledge, the list of publications below could be of help to readers:

BOOKS

Business @ the Speed of Thought: Using a Digital Nervous System
Bill Gates
Penguin Books, 1999

Competing for the Future
G Hamel, C K Prahalad
Harvard Business School Press, 1994

Experts in Organizations: a Knowledge-Based Perspective on Organizational Change
A Hatchuel and B Weil
Walter de Gruyter, 1995

Harvard Business Review on Breakthrough Thinking
Harvard Business School Press, 1999

Information, Organization and Power: Effective Management in the Knowledge Society
D E Zand
McGraw-Hill, 1981

Intellectual Capital
Thomas A Stewart
Nicholas Brealey Publishing, 1998

Organizational Learning and Competitive Advantage
B.Moingeon and A.Edmondson (eds)
Sage Publications, 1996

The Tacit Dimension
M Polanyi
Peter Smith Publications, 1983

The Knowledge Creating Company
I Nonaka, H Takeuchi;
Oxford University Press, 1995

Tacit Knowledge in Organizations
Philippe Baumard
Sage Publications, 1999

Articles

A Taxonomy of Knowledge Projects to Underpin Organizational Innovation and Competitiveness
A Braganza, C Edwards, R Lambert
Knowledge and Process Management, 6

The Knowledge-Creating Company
I Nonaka
Harvard Business Review, 1991

What is Chief Knowledge Officer?
M Earl, I Scott
Sloan Management Review, 40

Web sites

www.kmnews.com

www.mjm.co.uk

ceres.cibit.nl/index.html

www.media-access.com/resources.html